Four Super Seasons

WHAT HAPPENS IN FALL?

By Alex Appleby

Gareth Stevens
Publishing

Please visit our website, www.garethstevens.com. For a free color catalog of all our high-quality books, call toll free 1-800-542-2595 or fax 1-877-542-2596.

Library of Congress Cataloging-in-Publication Data

Appleby, Alex.
What happens in fall? / by Alex Appleby.
p. cm. — (Four super seasons)
Includes index.
ISBN 978-1-4824-0100-4 (pbk.)
ISBN 978-1-4824-0104-2 (6-pack)
ISBN 978-1-4824-0607-8 (library binding)
1. Autumn — Juvenile literature. I. Appleby, Alex. II. Title.
QB637.7 A66 2014
508.2—dc23

First Edition

Published in 2014 by
Gareth Stevens Publishing
111 East 14th Street, Suite 349
New York, NY 10003

Editor: Ryan Nagelhout
Designer: Andrea Davison-Bartolotta

Photo credits: Cover, p. 1 artjazz/Shutterstock.com; p. 5 maxslu/Shutterstock.com; p. 7 iofoto/Shutterstock.com; pp. 9, 11, 13, 15, 17, 19, 21, 23, 24 iStockphoto/Thinkstock.

Printed in the United States of America

CPSIA compliance information: Batch #CW14GS: For further information contact Gareth Stevens, New York, New York at 1-800-542-2595.

Fall is a super season!

It comes after summer.

Fall comes once a year.

It is also called autumn.

The weather starts to get colder.

People pick pumpkins!

Leaves start
to change colors.

Some turn orange.
Others turn red
or brown.

The leaves then fall
off trees.

Winter comes after fall.

Words to Know

leaves

pumpkins

Index